NEW YORK TRILOGY

ALSO BY PETER BALAKIAN

POETRY

*Father Fisheye*
*Sad Days of Light*
*Reply from Wilderness Island*
*Dyer's Thistle*
*June-Tree: New and Selected Poems, 1974–2000*
*Ziggurat*
*Ozone Journal*
*No Sign*

PROSE

*Theodore Roethke's Far Fields*
*Black Dog of Fate: A Memoir*
*The Burning Tigris: The Armenian Genocide and America's Response*
*Vise and Shadow: Essays on the Lyric Imagination, Poetry, Art, and Culture*

TRANSLATIONS

*Bloody News from My Friend: Poems by Siamanto* (with Nevart Yaghlian)
*Armenian Golgotha: A Memoir of the Armenian Genocide, 1915–1918* by Grigoris Balakian (with Aris Sevag)
*The Ruins of Ani* by Krikor Balakian (with Aram Arkun)

EDITED

*Ambassador Morgenthau's Story*
*A Slant of Light: Reflections on Jack Wheatcroft* (with Bruce Smith)

# NEW YORK TRILOGY

PETER BALAKIAN

The University of Chicago Press
Chicago and London

The University of Chicago Press, Chicago 60637
The University of Chicago Press, Ltd., London
© 2025 by The University of Chicago
"A-Train / Ziggurat / Elegy" © 2010 by The University of Chicago
"Ozone Journal" © 2015 by The University of Chicago
"No Sign" © 2022 by The University of Chicago
All rights reserved. No part of this book may be used or reproduced in any manner whatsoever without written permission, except in the case of brief quotations in critical articles and reviews. For more information, contact the University of Chicago Press, 1427 East 60th Street, Chicago, IL 60637.
Published 2025
Printed in the United States of America

34  33  32  31  30  29  28  27  26  25      1  2  3  4  5

ISBN-13: 978-0-226-84374-2 (paper)
ISBN-13: 978-0-226-84375-9 (ebook)
DOI: https://doi.org/10.7208/chicago/9780226843759.001.0001

Library of Congress Cataloging-in-Publication Data

Names: Balakian, Peter, 1951– author.
Title: New York trilogy / Peter Balakian.
Description: Chicago : The University of Chicago Press, 2025. | Includes bibliographical references.
Identifiers: LCCN 2025007524 | ISBN 9780226843742 (paperback) | ISBN 9780226843759 (ebook)
Subjects: LCGFT: Poetry.
Classification: LCC PS3552.A443 N49 2025 | DDC 811/.54—dc23/eng/20250307
LC record available at https://lccn.loc.gov/2025007524

♾ This paper meets the requirements of ANSI/NISO Z39.48-1992 (Permanence of Paper).

Authorized Representative for EU General Product Safety Regulation (GPSR) queries: Easy Access System Europe—Mustamäe tee 50, 10621 Tallinn, Estonia, gpsr.requests@easproject.com
Any other queries: https://press.uchicago.edu/press/contact.html

To the memory of my aunts
GLADYS AND LUCILLE AROOSIAN
who first showed me the great City

It grieves me to watch the end of any good work to which
men have given so much thought and skill.

SIR LEONARD WOOLLEY, *Excavations at Ur*

\*

Take a flat brush and work it till there are two hairs left.

ARSHILE GORKY

# CONTENTS

*Author's Note*

ix


**ONE**

A-Train / Ziggurat / Elegy

3


**TWO**

Ozone Journal

37


**THREE**

No Sign

69


*Notes on the Text*

93

AUTHOR'S NOTE

*New York Trilogy* is comprised of three long, multisequence poems that appeared in my last three books, *Ziggurat* (2010), *Ozone Journal* (2015), and *No Sign* (2022). I wrote each poem as one part of a long poem in three sections. *New York Trilogy* explores one man's journey, from the late 1960s into the early twenty-first century, a journey that evolves from a series of experiences and events, many of which are set in New York and the onlooking New Jersey Palisades. The life and imagination of the persona are impacted by various historical events: the Armenian Genocide, Hiroshima, the Vietnam War, the AIDS epidemic, 9/11, the US war in Iraq, and the geo-climate crisis. The persona's perspective is shaped by an oscillation between past and present, where history and political violence intersect with intimate relationships, love and loss, and the persona's lifelong engagements with literature, art, and music.

Jersey Cliffs<br>November 1, 2024

# ONE

# A-TRAIN / ZIGGURAT / ELEGY

1.

The tender head of the he-goat (on the cover)
stares through the branches of a golden tree,

and I'm just moving on a system of fuses,
while the fruit stands of Spanish Harlem fly above,

and even now remembering when we were here
after Nixon waved goodbye and rose in the chopper.

Even now seeing it through the double glass
as *Ur of the Chaldees* (revised and updated)

*Sir Leonard Woolley's Excavations at Ur*
flares on the yellow cover in the momentary dark

that wrapped our bodies, up all night, like violent paint
on the sheets; like the broken fire escape of our building.

At 125th, the guy next to me reading *Another Country*;
the white guy passed out in a suit and a brown bag.

The steel screeches the tracks, and the vaults light up.

2.

To Woolley, the Crash and Wall Street
were a Fata Morgana of palms shattered in ice.

He paid baksheesh to the locals and they kept digging—
baked clay and gypsum

Woolley loved cow dung, mud plaster huts: the world from bottom up.

"We found a clay figurine of a pig,
spindle-whorls of baked clay prove that thread was spun here."

*

In the last days of Babylon
a mathematician gave zero a name,
not far from where Woolley dug.

No great thing comes without a curse, said Sophocles—
So Zero = hollow circle = cylinder seal—
"Skulls and seeds and all good things are round" (Nabokov).


3.

You made his lines, which were opaque as ashes,
seem clear as our confusion.

("the diagonal black's a broken body")

it was after the show, we walked from Tung-Lai Shun
to the Bowery to the Bridge and back.

"I like bridges," Franz Kline said, "if people want to see bridges
in my lines that's good."

And when we fell into the shadow of the morning,
why did we stop talking, after all, after all of it, after everything.

You disappeared on the train reading Merleau-Ponty
I got lost in Queens on the E.


4.

I ran mail a whole summer down Greenwich and West.
Before it even started, before we roamed Radio Row
for 78s of Ellington and the Blanton Trio,

before the yin-yang of real estate
under the Kensett skies over the river,
the wrecking balls took Radio Row down:

florists, groceries, record shops, restaurants
the whole mid-century slid into a pit
and the sun made gothic trees of the falling windows.

Out of *res ipsa loquitur*.
Out of Port Authority and Chase,
Rockefeller and Tobin,
the Twin Towers rose from the garbage.

5.

But to Woolley it wasn't Iraq, it wasn't post-empire or Faisal's kingdom,
it was precise digging into the beginning,
as if the piece of the snake's tail that was swallowed by its mouth
made the full circle of history.

"All the bodies lay on their backs, rigidly extended: hands crossed below the stomach,
the graves, dug into the silt were"

—after the flood: decayed brick, ashes,
potsherds, flints, clay figurines—

I used to think of post-diluvian as theoretical.
But if you ask: what became of the Sumerians?

"It grieves me to watch the end of any good work
to which men have given so much thought and skill."

*

Woolley agreed with Duchamp:
America's greatest art was its plumbing
and NYC the summation of sewage pipes and sinks,

some of which join here in the 59th Street Station
where we're stuck, and before the lights go out I can see
the pale blue and white tiles glistening like Lucca della Robbias.

6.

I watched it half-drugged by the sun off the West Street pier:

"First, there was the construction of the core or rectangular elevator-service area where all the interior columns were clustered together. From the core, the floor system reached in a clear and unobstructed clean sweep to the exterior wall. . . . Although few tenants subsequently took full advantage of the dramatic interior layout potential, the fact remains that the architecture offered great possibilities. It was at the core that the giant kangaroo cranes lifted the steel from the outside."


7.

We met on a cold morning
when the women were gathering dew.
START AGAIN: We met at a party in a loft on Greene St.
in the no-gravity of Barsamian's big canvases;
post-Magritte you called it; a vagina and no head, breasts but no limbs.

The red wine was Chilean, this was after Allende and Neruda.
I watched your mouth in the dark reflection of the window
beyond which the light of the towers glared the black red.

But still the need to ask:
Who wrapped the day in nectar?
Who cracked the sun over the hedges?
Who saw the light flare off the towers at dusk?

What's loss if not an open grave
where the heart is eaten by worms.

8.

Woolley thought the original Ur was built on a low mound
rising only just above the surrounding swampland—

"Here all traces of human activity ceased and we were at the bottom of
 Mesopotamia."

*

Among the many things the Sumerians handed down
is the story of a flood, cf. *Gilgamesh*,

and after that, kingship was sent down from on high
so civilization could start again.

For Woolley it was a tweed jacket and vest in the Iraqi sun, mid-winter
 evenings,
two martinis up—his supply from Harrods.


9.

1/30/06

"John Hendricks and the cameraman Al Diehl
were standing up in the back hatch of an Iraqi armored vehicle,
not a Humvee, something 'softer,' taping the patrol."

I was driving back to Hamilton
in snow on Rt. 17, and the words came
like distortion of sound from the dashboard:

"combined operation with the Iraqi army,"
"coalition forces," "soft targets."
IED jammers, wireless—embedded with the 4th Infantry—

"If you are going to cover the Iraqi forces
you have to be with them."
Your students always live

in their seats, their faces smooth,
teeth shining, John '83, bristling
rugby-energy in his chair.

"John was bleeding from the head;
'Am I alive? Don't tell Ann.'"


10.

And when I think of I/then we/then back to I—
in that spot where before I knew you, I watched the ditch dug:
the mist and silt on my arms
running past the hulls of Cunard and Chilean.

"From within this 'bathtub excavation' came the detritus of early European settlement, for this part of the Hudson was first used as a garbage dump and then filled in to extend the island westward.

Burned and capsized vessels and anchors,
clay pipes, hand blown bottles—drinking glasses, salt-glaze pots, shoes,
bones of countless animals, cannon balls, a litho of Grover Cleveland."


11.

We kept going around and around and at the zero spot

the hole became a black hole in which you,
you had to confess your past, and so there it was,

was again; the marsh reeds were high and we were in them
in the lemony light as the trucks on the Pike drilled past us.

And now the lights out and the subway car steaming with bodies,
the stink of the bourbon and cigarettes of the guy passed out next to me—
a silver flash on the facing track, then dark.


12.

9/21/03

All day the campus floated in light,
the pond bronze with carp

not mud-brown late-March clotted debris—
but darting, transparent, cutting past

a large gold or walleye; trees
of riotous color left late summer in the curb.

The granite stone of Lawrence Hall
glittered through the elms,

and lawn rolled as we walked
down slope to the rugby field,

close to where Ann was chasing the twins as
they tumbled down the hill.

You had returned with clips
of the Al Qaeda camp in Pakistan

where you lived for weeks
among the poor and angry.

"Death to America" on school walls.
Poppy head and gladiator. White Satan.

The war had just started
as you returned to the City

to your new job as the nightly news anchor.
But the images called you back.

Camouflage of the embedded—
the Humvee tracks, acronyms for Iraq.


13.

Yamasaki made the towers to withstand the crash of a 747,
the vortex, the phantom, the lateral-winds,

exterior walls carrying the vertical loads and wind

and they came: exterior columns from Seattle,
beams from Alabama, trusses from Texas, columns from Pittsburgh, floor
    assemblies from Newark.

PONYA WTC 213.00 236B 4-9 558 35 TONS

Under the cranes, hydraulic lifts, guy wires, derricks,
I sat with a couple Sabretts and a Coke,

the ozone blotting out Jersey.

14.

The flood left silt and minerals
which Woolley's men sifted like black flour.

And then it came—
("Only the Gods can live forever"),

and Gilgamesh was left to wander the earth,
friendless, looking for God.

It swallowed everything,
though sky and water are still emblems of the possible,
alluvium, crushed fish bones, pummeled rocks.

*

O house of heaven rising
O foundation of earth
O elemental zig zag

City of the moon god Nanna,
home of Abraham, wind-bitten badlands of the soul;
water-marked buttes, blades of hawk wings, heart-surge of the body.

Today it's Tell al-Muqayyar where
Agatha Christie, who spent time with Woolley, set *Murder in Mesopotamia*.

You forget that Nebuchadnezzar inherited the region a millennium later.

You forget because it's just an excavation now,
like my mind when it blanks into itself,

like the horizon when it goes black and the flame
of one oil refinery flickers out at the Syrian border

where I once picked Armenian bones out of the dirt.



15.

We held out for Valentine and Virgin Mary.
In cold hard light. Worm Moon and no sap in trees,
there was blood on our sheets.

The pipes were frozen.
Chinese kites stuck on wires.

We painted each other in the I-love-you dyes of
expectation and faith,

each red letter stamped *jagad-a-krese*—
in Armenian: written on your forehead:

Fate. Armenian nuance:
it's on you, others see it—you don't.

In the end I didn't come through for you,

and the end was the beginning of late February:
entitled, luscious, leap-year.

Here's to life. *Genat-sut*.
Here's to March, Mars,
God who protects the land.

16.

3/1/06

An email came like a blink on the screen after midnight.
I was up emailing friends in Beirut who were describing
the twisted steel that was rusting in the markets.

"This is like being in a circle of Dante's *Inferno*,"
Ann wrote, "We're here at the VA hospital.
John has the best doctors possible.

He's speaking—though in several languages,
Chinese, French, sounds just come pell mell.

The kids are talking with their father—everyone holding together.
The support of so many people gives us strength."


17.

Etemenanki—tower of Babel/
*Babuli*: gate to God

chthonic zig zag of hubris
(not far from Ur), at the heart of a great city,

echoing the question Prometheus asked:
does God have a right to heaven alone?

    *

Pieter Brueghel had it all wrong:
there was solid masonry in the middle of the Tower,
a winding path circling the eight towers,
baked brick glued with asphalt

only to have the builders
wake up confused or confounded

and after came the poets:
*balal* in Hebrew: a writer full of puns
a scatterer of language—

signifying the fact: put down your tools
and walk elsewhere—diaspora: meaning

polyglot mountains and the lakes of many continents

(in Armenian we say: *garod* meaning longing—sickness after exile, need for the
   beloved).


18.

I follow the cochineal thread of the skyline,
a single weft pulled by a crow's beak
over the high-rises of Fort Lee.


19.

Days I sank in the rubble, and the noise
drove out of my head the most basic words

like now when we're mute and
the wheels of the train drown out the noise in my head.

Below the B-2 level
the multimillion line Nynex switching station

generator/air-conditioning/giant computer—
was filling up the hole left by the garbage of history.

I couldn't imagine a silicon brain
or hear the humming of the inaudible frequencies

of magnetic core memory
of the integrated circuits of a capacitor—

some days I found places along the pier
where I sat and went blank

(this was before Ginsberg
introduced me to meditation),

staring at the tugs pushing the freight barges
toward Staten Island till red merged with black

and the black became a point of no return
like you fading out of sight on the pier


20.

and black hole of loneliness rose up in me.

And now the shaking train starts to pull out of Columbus Station.

"Omens," said Ovid, "are wont to wait upon beginnings."

You said:

*Poets are paranoid, apocalyptic,*

*style-drunk, sense-lusters, hypochondriacs.*


21.

The creosote vaults at 42nd
covered in Day-Glo neon Pollock
over the girders of "peace but fuck you anyway"

the man reading Baldwin getting out,
and a drunk guy who could be dead slumped against
the window scratched: *Fallujah.*


22.

On the street I heard that the Indians
were like cold-blooded dancers at high altitudes.

Mohawks who had come down from Canada.

I watched them glide with hot rivets
and cold steel into the azure of near oblivion.

Some days they disappeared in light
as if the narrow beams of air came undone

and they floated between steel and blue like lost angels.

My head spiraled from the fumes of coffee and
yellow bulls, red cranes, green trucks, pale blue drilling rigs

bull's liver; gooseneck; clam shell; orange peels;
192,000 tons of steel—


23.

I was beginning to see Woolley—after the inexorable, rotting earth began
to sink into itself, after the metal and the bones disappeared,

after the Treaty divvied up the Arab world
and the latitudes were lubricious

spilling over Basra where J. E. Taylor found
his mound of pitch and inscriptions of the nameless ruin.

Ubaid, Uruk, Jamdat Nasr—
the weeds—scribes and skeletons.


24.

Just before the lights went black
the silver-Pullman-flash of another train

with the flag on every car now,
glowing before it goes dark again
somewhere past 23rd.


25.

I loved your love of myth and ritual.
I loved reading Eliade with you on the train.

The uroboric windows hugged the car,
the spring rain washed away the serpent's tail.

Still I love you as I write this,
though our moment passed like Ash Wednesday

when you returned with the sign on your head.
Everything went black and silent

like that Saturday when Jesus lay in the tomb
before the apotheosis we waited for all spring long.

I loved how you took me down Pentecostal
without restraint or faith

into the dark vaults lower than the 4th Street Station.
No mythological bullshit here

you were the realest of the real
with your mad black hair and your crushing childhood.

Your lips of plum and turpentine
were signifier and signified,

the crêpe de Chine, the lace, the chinoiserie,
the strange clock your father brought from Thrace

kept ticking at us as if we were in Attica.


26.

2/15/06

Some days I heard John's voice in my head in
the way a poem wants to enter the other

for a glimpse of the unutterable
and from the fragments in Ann's email:

*like headlights in fog*
*floating down the well*

*the Blackhawk chopping sand-wind*

*the tank-grate-metal-hit*

*the snake crawls along the jaw*
*then out the hole of the back.*


27.

It was true: The Armenians got to Jesus first,
at least officially, ahead of Rome,

and this devastated you because you had
believed all those truths of catechism

all that dogma which spelled backwards
is humiliation and extravagance

the kind of thing Fellini made you see
in *Roma* and we left the Angelika laughing

at your confirmation dress and your mother's
anxious rosary you carried in your purse.

28.

Who is the other who
floats between what you see

and what is there:
think of the other going silent,

screen fuzz smoke,
hours away on TV.

Came as dumb smoke

into my house.
The jade plant leaves,

tongue of the cat,
pan on the stove,

the cardamom and clove
moved in their currents.

I look. You look. We look.

Outside the sky was searing blue,
honeysuckle wafting through

the screen door.
The Towers were melting down.

There was nowhere to go.
Sat down. Got up.

Stared at my laptop.
Walked around.

No phone service.
The cell's dead too.


29.

"Dalí once told me my work was related to John of the Cross.
I've never read him," Kline said, "I wouldn't know."

You thought melting clocks were a cheap gimmick
like most of surrealism

and Dalí: hyper, overwrought, esthete.
But Kline caught Dr. J and Nijinsky in a stroke—

he saw the truth about us in diagonal slashes.


30.

Days I was almost fired; checks late to the bank;
mail in piles by the meter machine because the grillages transfixed me—

twenty-eight grillages supporting the columns of the elevator core of the
    North Tower,
core box-shaped columns and box-beam framing.

Who had ever heard of anything like this?

A gang of workers guided the grillage onto the concrete slab or footing
seventy feet below street level, foundation to erection, each one:
thirty-four tons, fifteen feet long, eleven feet wide, and seven feet high.

"Domenico Delicarpini, a thirty-year-old, $140-a-week laborer, married
and the father of four children"—plunged thirty feet on May 15, 1969,
when some planking gave way. Fractured his neck and spinal cord, will never
work again; awarded $500,000 by the State Supreme Court in Bronx in a case
against the Port Authority and Tishman.



31.

The drum roll of wheels over tracks—
my head synced with the streak

of signs: Euclid Ave. Blue C.
8th Ave. Local World Trade Center (the words still there)

against the black and white ticking of the tiles
dissolving into neon dust—and I asked



32.

where were we going as the rhododendrons fell into themselves
and the park seemed to levitate on the fume.

Peachwood strips will drive out evil spirits.
We drove the brown Corolla to Rhinebeck for the weekend.

The ash and spruce were resinous in our throats;
you set out pots of sedum, dumb-cakes, dreaming bannocks,

at high noon you broke an egg in a bowl
and read the fantastic shapes of the flowing whites.

We lit our fire of bones; baun = beacon,
*Bane* = fire for banishing evil.

Screw all things civic and patriotic
you wrote in big letters on a note pad

after seeing Agnew's plastic face
rise like a balloon on the screen.

Stonehenge and Tiahuanaco.
Bloom watching Gerty McDowell

as the roman candles poured their fire.
Read it to me again.


33.

The first incoming message arrived over a direct
teleprinter circuit, a confirmation of a sale of spice

from Ceylon to Colombia, 9:54 a.m.
EST Tuesday, December 15, 1970,
tenth and eleventh floors of the North Tower.

Those mornings I lived on gravity, wind, and fear,
the observation elevators, sky lobbies,
glass-sides ran faster than a subway.

Inside the glass box
I looked back at myself
as in a fun-house room where

each plane shattered
any idea of the whole,
though the parts were more than the sum

—the way the style
of the sundial projects the shadow,
the way sunyata knows all entities

are empty. Was this why
the Mayan symbol for zero
was a tattooed man in a necklace

with his head thrown back?

*

I watched the pioneer firms
unload into the unfinished space of the Tower
as the Hudson sun poured down the core.

On the street it was Christmas,
the scotch was pouring at the White Horse,
the homeless guys in boxes

stretched out on visible corners
in empty lots and church porticos.

It was hardly Thoreau's open-air house,
but it was a strange brew of wind and light,
clanging metal and teleprinter circuits.

At the topping out ceremony on the 23rd floor
the iron workers soldered a flag
to a thirty-six-foot-long four-ton column

hoisted by a kangaroo crane
and then it came—
a thirty-foot Christmas tree

on a three-story-high exterior wall section
on the southeast corner of the building.
The regulation was three cans of beer per guest.



34.

The drum roll of wheels over tracks.
The streak of Euclid Ave. Blue C.

8th Ave. Local World Trade Center
(still up) against the black and white ticking of the tiles.


35.

For the underworld God the Sumerians harvested grain
on the naked ground—120 degrees—
the same color as Kline's white.

"The Ziggurat is a peculiar feature of Mesopotamian architecture . . .
it is still not certain whether the ziggurats of the Ur III period were the
expressions of a new religious concept or whether such buildings raised by
Ur-Nammu in various of his cities were merely the final stage
of a long architectural development."


36.

Gazing at Franz Kline—

black bites back—bites the head off
the illusion so that white is

not the empty face, the apparition,
but the joyful stone, the sheet of Jesus.

Not the lost man in Lapland,
the white sea, the buffalo robe,

but the belly of any fish—
the canvas gaze,

whatever opalescent film
the oyster brings to surface.


37.

Between *Bananas* and *Annie Hall*
there was a big hole in the window

south of Coentis Slip, south of Warhol,
where we walked our thousand miles

never jumping from the plank.
"Ford to City: Drop Dead"

was the stuffed insulation
in our half-done loft south of Franklin,

where we heard the hidden fifths of Philip Glass
rise like isotopic rings up the shaft

of the invisible elevator we rode
into the ecstatic, garbage-filled glow

of purple-red as it lit up
the McAllister tugs

and the barely visible birds
that followed in the Ferry.


38.

Everything was tangled up in blue.
Seeping glaze on the Delft jug,

liquefaction of the Virgin's silk
as it spread in Titian's cobalt

to a fleshy embrace and the green meadows
in the distance fade to hammered light.

Light we pulled into a string of glass
that seeped out of the long vibration

of Miles's *Blue in Green*
like slow time in the empty lot

after soot and rain and rush,
the Ferry out of sight,

my bones electric with the hum
of the cable of the Bridge at 3 a.m.

and the dying lights of the Bowery.
Bill Evans making the rain thin

to a beam of haze before the
horn comes back from under water.

39.

When the subway lights came back on—
the white Pumas on the ad strip flashed

onto my page—*Joda Por Una* Bud Light
glared under the white *Osama* slashed.


40.

*We could have gone together.*
Beads of carnelian, lapis, glazed fruit, gold.

*The look in the mirror sent me away.*
The ruins of houses and the cemetery.

*When is it ever the right time?*
Plano-convex brick in our archeological jargon—

*Why did Apollo give the car to Phaeton?*
Layers of debris from burnt buildings covered from red to sooty black—

*It was a hell of a fire.*
Lumps of clay plastered over the stoppers of store jars—

*Will the end come like this?*
Seal impressions found in the rubbish strata with the tablets.

41.

The black comes down on us.
The Inuit understood this.
They fished in total darkness.

All December sky and water
converged and they learned to catch by feel.
There was firelight and they loved in it.


42.

Flaring new gingko leaves,
island of tulips smearing by us,

*(O strongest you in the hour of danger, in crisis! O truer than steel!)*

and we get out here under the deafening chopper NYPD
the sky brilliant as the yellow cab

*How your soft opera music changed . . .*

we can't hear each other; in the deafening silence
"the poem becomes desperate conversation" (Celan)

*Sleepless amid her ships, her houses, her incalculable wealth*

your father remembered
the pilots falling from the white heat o of the Japanese sun

the chrysanthemum singeing into smoke rings on the postage stamps
stuffed in his bomber jacket

*O superb! O Manhattan, my own, my peerless!*

the stretcher disappeared into the chopper.
The flags—a blur around the UN.


43.

Even if we met at junctures elegiac (Hart Crane). RE-DO.
Even if the windows opened to techno trance not far from where Val Solanis
    shot Warhol
as the strobes faded out; even if we lived in the cold-water flat
of our embracing names and the train shook the lath and the mirrors

I sat all day on a broken bench till you returned.


44.

I would sing now on that lyre
decomposed but for the brilliant golden
head of the he-goat and the braided

lapis beard carved so finely
you can feel the roots
and the spiral braids come alive

in your hand just as now the sound
of those strings in the half-life of the carbon
purrs in the isotopic air

of those hecatombs where Woolley's black light
scanned a silver tumbler, fluted and chased,
in some color that's gone

45.

as the rings
unspool out of the whiteness
that hovers on the canopy

of the higher buildings
of lower Broadway over the
underpass to the Holland tunnel

as the trace of my passing
leaves nothing but

the phosphor
of some thought that twines
the air as the body sleeks—

and the day comes
with its faint industrial orange
glow and sun on river.

# TWO

# OZONE JOURNAL

1.

I woke to CFCs humming out of coils.

I woke to a compressor in my head
and the compressor in the wall that made cool air come out of the vents—

couldn't sleep—downloaded photos of the day,
to stare at them, as if the sky were something I could breathe in:

not good times by the sea, but—desert-blue and cracked ground,

some tumbleweed blowing into my jeans;
green signs of Arabic letters looked like beautiful tributaries,

as they faded out along a road going to the Iraqi border,

where oil refineries were firing on the horizon,
where a border is a road: ending and beginning.


2.

All day I was digging Armenian bones out of the Syrian desert

with a TV crew that kept ducking the Mukhabarat
who trailed us in jeeps and at night joined us

for arak and grilled goat under colored pennants and cracked lights
in cafés where piles of herbs glistened back at me.

I passed out from sun and arak and camel jokes

in a massive hotel, my room opened to the Euphrates
that was churning in the moonlight.


3.

When I woke I was dreaming back to the '80s on Riverside Drive
where Ani was born on a bright spring day,

in a decade of money and velvet when the plastic voice of Sinatra
floated through fern bars where we lounged

with wine spritzers and lemon-drop martinis.
It was silver palette and more than cuisine

with its encoded sense of ending
and the smoked sable at Barney Greengrass

where we took Ani for brunch
on Sunday when the morning was lit up and open.


4.

dreaming back to days
(why here on the black Euphrates at 4:00 a.m.?)

after our life went up in a blue flame as the gas jet died
and—we were gone to each other—

the walls silent and the floorboards echoed;
the U-Haul came and my books got rained on—

and the flags were rippling for Saint Gennaro.
Thisbe and Pyramus disappeared as myth and symbol
and that summed it up.


5.

Those days (no dream) the squeaky cassette going—
on Jerry in Riverdale. When I arrived the sky was graphed
through phone wires and Amtrak cables.

I was sitting beneath shelves of uncut masters—
the 78s of 1940 when Jerry cut the modern LP
and found the lost Hot Jazz of the '20s—

I was staring at hanging Armenian rugs and the river glare
on a photo of Miles Davis—almost liquid in the sepia emulsion

of 1947 when the smoke spiraled into Three Deuces on 52nd
at a table with Sterling Brown and Gillespie and Jerry—

and he put it (in his hammered speech), "John Hammond
was so hated by the musicians, Miles cut him out of the photo and pasted
Dizzy in—but that was before I got Miles interested in John Cage."


6.

By noon I was leaning on the cotton white hospital wall,
gazing at the islands of purple lesions on
David's slightly swollen leg, the edema rising

in his groin, the sheets strewn and the IV
dripping blue down the snaking plastic tube.

My year of magical thinking looped down
the drain of my brain: "Take care, cousin."

I blew him a kiss,


7.

before I was back at the English department table,

feeling the postmortem of the modern:
the paradigm critique essential but the artifact
thrown out with the bathwater—

over-fetishizing indeterminacy,
or depressed expression of late capitalism?

Get Foucault and Trilling in bed—
give peace a chance.

Gorky said, take a flat brush
and work it till there are two hairs left.


8.

Light comes diffuse out of itself over the Euphrates
from the hotel room veranda—irrigated farmland/yellow tint/
veins running through furrows/snaking green patches—

9.

and I see David's eyes flat and glassy;
his voice through Xanax

was a silk kerchief through a ring.
Memory was focus, detail, the thing—

*the way sun lit up our brownstone—*

*the way a good Burgundy was a whiff when the cork pops*
*and the air is Tiffany and evening comes*

*with its mix and synthesized backing track.*

*Pigeons flew into porch lanterns*
*and the spring synth notes of Donna Summer,*

*as the cold and hot pianos melted into riot bombs of*
*strobes and the dust of white powder:*


10.

When I walked under the canopy of the Ansonia
I saw your hand in the restoration of
the turreted copper and the beaux arts angels,

the mansard roof floated in the ultra rays,

where you worked in the early '80s on the running
frieze and the cornices

while down on the sidewalk, everyone was buffed up on glistening
shops of leather, tiers of mangos, apples, honeydew.

At night Ani slept as if we were still together.
Her breathing calmed the saw that spits the air.


11.

Gray-yellow light over the river;
got a train to Riverdale and sat with Jerry over

Armenian coffee as he sorted through papers and photos
and one of Billy H. at Three Deuces and Jerry put it this way:

"We were there till the early light came into the club
and Miles was shaking like a paralytic"

*Cultivate in yourself a grand similarity*
*with the chaos of the surrounding ether;*

*unloose your mind; set your spirit free;*
*be still as if you had no soul* (Cage)

"Miles laughed, then passed out,

that sense of nothing—ness came
alive when we did the *Blue* sessions...."


12.

Breakfast in the van: muhammara, fig jam,
thin pita-like soft parchment;

I'm eating earth and air as I fold
it over cracked green olives—

military vehicles shedding rust—
khaki camouflage and the Assad-
faced facades looking back at us.


13.

I watched David's Buddhist
gaze as he imagined how

the body turned on itself and the virus
spiked its protein into T cells

(he was drawing on napkins: CD4/CD8)

"That summer we complained of coughs,
numb skin in spots in early evening

when the Lux filled up and the homeless came to Gray's Papaya—"

He kept talking through the beep of the IV;
at noon the nurses wheeled in some trays.


14.

On the days when the rings on our fingers hurt,
I drifted into the white noise of the crowd
on the turned-up TV; no need for Stoli—

the field cam gaze brought me the dazzling green
white lines/foul pole/second-base glistening,
the green transfixing like money.

The heroes haunting us after the game—
the idea of glory rubbing off

on our shirts like angel dust;
anyone lost in the crowd

is born again in the afterimage
of buoyancy and beer—

the ego dissolving into victory over death
for a day, or a moment of certainty,

as Camus once put it:

"If only once it could be said: *this is clear*—
then all would be saved."


15.

Speeding by al-Raqqah, appearing, disappearing—
the idea of Babylon, Assyria, Sumer:
an abstraction of sun on water—

toward Margadeh—smell of sandstorm rising—
caves appearing, disappearing into huts of light.

16.

The present kept sliding into David's past,
unraveling through drip-drugs and sedatives.

I heard a version of the Upper West at a moment
when history was an image caught in a pincer:

morning was blood orange on Columbus Ave.
evening was a rum punch and then

a riot of Quiana collars/blow and poppers
arms and legs of Jell-O in the stairwells
where Calvin Klein disappeared like a holy ghost,

and out there in the American day—Terrence Malick's light
spread on the libidinal wheat and rutted prairie—

that was the '70s: post-Nixon
euphoria, pre-Khomeini inflation of the soul
over the Williamsburg Bridge at midday

the full-throated wobbly sax
of Sonny Rollins when everyone was
a bachelor with a PhD in anthro or comp lit,


17.

and then I was hunched under the celeb photos on the wall
over an absurd pile of pastrami at the Carnegie, and a snippet
fell out of my notebook: "The measurements onboard the *Nathaniel B. Palmer*

showed that a one-hour exposure to light that is similar
to the sun under the ozone hole is enough to completely stop all
photosynthetic activity of the plankton."

No plankton = no world: who can take in the dread—

and I'm already late to pick up Ani at dance class.


18.

Jerry believed what the Greeks believed: sound had color

and what Miles said: "The softer you play, the stronger it gets"

when I got home my daughter's voice was skidding
along the fluctuating magnetic signal of the answering machine—

loneliness droned me to the beep, lulled me to sleep


19.

before I woke to hammered silver air over the river—

fish-eye sun—irascible, hardtack, scarred, and varnished,

ozone: major factor in making life on earth possible;
$O_3$—allotropic, oxidizing, disinfectant, poisonous;
pale blue gas, sharp, irritating—ignited by UV rays.

20.

Obsessive angles of light off stone in the Syrian desert,
5:00 a.m., camera crew: M. and B. brilliant
making the narrative hang in the/blind

/white/punctum

boom mike dangles/a huge mouth—
in sun—


21.

the morning sun trance taking me back to
T cells floating in the elevator at Saks,
spikes of protein/genome invasion—

between Chernobyl and Bhopal
AIDS became gossip, evasion, denial.


22.

We were walking our Friday ritual
over the GW, the lights of Midtown burning—

we were buzzed on nothing,
the nothing of the night sky half-smogged
with wavering lights on the cables,

buzzed on water from a wooden bowl,
a liquor never brewed—

I keep saying it, even if the lines
were from the greats of the American sublime,
because our special wine never grew in the belly of the grape.


23.

When the driver stopped for arak at a gas station the color of
pomegranates/smeared plums/Syrian lavender/
I was texting Ani back in Boston—the send-icon spinning nowhere.


24.

On Sundays I came to the hospital with café au lait and choreg—

David was all memory as if the Madeleine were floating in tea:

outside of a jazz club in Beyoğlu, Turkey—he told me:

*Alan (the love of my life) was ranting (why there, why then?)*

*about the wall that came down*
*at Stonewall, before we all/*

*and then/and how/*

*the Humpty Dumpty faggot cops, handcuffed women,*
*Van Ronk and company too.*

*Fairies weren't supposed to fight back;*

*someone doused the bar with lighter fluid—*
*the street was Jackson Pollock smashed,*
*pay phones toilets jukebox cigarette machines—*

*we hung our peacock-embellished texts*
*on the graffiti-ripped plaster of Christopher Street*

*spectral emanations rose off the curb.*

*And here we were standing under the Turkish street light,*
*charred lamb in the air;*
*we chugged our scotch and*

*and back we went inside the club with*
*a couple of Kurdish guys*

*and later near dawn set out to find*
*the wall on the Bosphorus*

*where our family house once stood.*


25.

When the streaming light came over the buttes and oil towers
the Euphrates looked pewter—

and then the sound of planes pealed
over the Iraqi border—

where the green zones turned into car bombs,
blast-wall T-hit barbed-wire;

the Tigris was fire and Babylonian bricks;
through the chained acres of ruined silt
sheep were driven into the Kurdish north.


26.

We strolled over the East River,
as the ultraviolet rays split off chlorine atoms,

Ani wrapped in infant pink and white;

at 161st we found the bleachers
where the lights blinded the moths.

Dominican boys ran from scalpers/MLB
cowhide on the hand and heart—

Later, walking back over the Macombs Bridge—
chlorine monoxide left us lighter.


27.

"Down at Café Bohemia,"

Jerry was talking slow now/the light going fast
into the violet-gray river air (I'd been there for hours),

"we started recording"—

(my primitive cassette recorder was squeaking)

"in late '55—after the third session,
Miles said, 'anything goes, but only when nothing is taken as the basis'—

sounded like baked-over Cage to me:

a source for the cool, for Miles Ahead,
for his fastidious dragged air."


28.

Women along the roadside in—burqa—
*wrapped in black*, I thumbed it on my iPhone.

Past the massive walls of the Aleppo Citadel,
*wrapped in black*.

I dozed in the throaty dust of Arabic and Armenian
coming off cell phones in the front seat.


29.

Memory was someone's history: private, political, social—
so I remember the ginkgo twisted out of the sidewalk by our door,

second nature of light—light of spectrum and love—
light of Grünewald's great halo in the sky

blew through us as we walked across Sheep Meadow

just outside the violet end of infrared at sunset.

Ani kept demanding soft ice cream.
I carried her on my shoulders till dark.


30.

News kept pouring off the telex color screen blur iPhone,

old *Chaldean bricks washed into the Tigris*,
the cylinder seals—pieces of Ur gone—

and I'm still trying to text Ani in Boston.


31.

I walked in with two coffees in Styrofoam—still black over
the Hudson, a stalled-out Amtrak car under the rail lamp—

Jerry hoarse and whispering:

"I'm here—here—because of ninety-two bales of rugs that sailed out of
    Tabriz.

And by the time we moved to 3rd Ave. the sound was coming
    through warps
and wefts. A man stood on a tenement roof in the black air;

I heard the impulse shoot through water towers and fire escapes;
Fats Waller was clear from WLW Cincinnati after midnight;

my parents spoke another language in another room;
the Persian tiles glistened // the floor was flower hieroglyphs—"

32.

The green zone was flitting like digital dots in the rearview mirror,

the camera crew got hold of severe/soft/breaking/light at 5:00 a.m.

our vans drifted past some ruins and caves.

33.

Back then—we woke to exhaust fumes.
You came in with espresso and a bowl of berries.

By noon I could see the yellow haze on the Jersey side.
Bach's cantata in B-flat minor in the cassette,
we lounged under the greenhouse-sky, the UVBs hacking
at the acids and oxides and then I could hear the difference

between an oboe and a bassoon
at the river's edge under cover—
trees breathed in our respiration,

there was that something on the other side of the river,
something both of us were itching toward—

radical bonds were broken, history became science.
We were never the same.

34.

*To articulate the past historically* (as Walter B. put it), after midnight on

the D from Flushing, crammed between two kids—

*does not mean to recognize it the way it really was.*

"I can feel it in the air tonight, O Lord," the boom box at the stop at 59th—

*it means to seize hold of a memory as it flashes up at the moment of danger—*


35.

Back then we walked through overburnished hanging wares
into CNN and Nintendo.

Ani and her friends huddled over icons on a Mac

and the real became MS-DOS
chipped into the ministry

of arbitrage in the middle of Reaganism
in some elusive embrace in our new stuffed interiors.


36.

"On a freezing night in January (I was 17) helping Benny Goodman
who was playing for the Spanish Loyalists at Columbus Circle,

I crammed Lionel Hampton's xylophone and Gene Kruppa's drums into a taxi,

cut my hand on the xylophone; the blood froze on the keys all the way up 6th Ave.
Inside a makeshift room I was the Jew, the Armenian, the horn-rimmed kid from

prep school they thought was him, and they handed me a glass; they called for him who
hadn't arrived, and so I raised a glass and shouted 'Muerte a Franco!'

The room peeled with joy, the lights smoked up, the grappa burned me down,

Peggy Lee appeared out of the smoke; down the edge of a dark wall bodies
drifted through space, the winds hustled four to the bar—we were the red hordes

turning Catalonia into the American thing, into the mistral where the guns drowned
in the erratic tempo of waves, into the arms and legs that wrapped me up all night—"


37.

While our friends in Tribeca were buzzed
on other stuff

we were high on the ripe river air of Friday nights—
as the bird-dazzled clouds floated over the GW

our belief—in Dylan Thomas's thunderous cadences
like backed-up water let loose over a barricade

as we went down by the riverbank
and were mad for the atmosphere,

the collision, the sweetest of entries,

the long pulsations before the sun broke
in our heads like Rothko's yellow coating the flax—

under the Palisades at the Boat Basin
looking up at the Bridge, at the Deco girders,

dreaming of the Algonquin and Edmund Wilson
in 1930 when the river was bridgeless.

Down there on the bank—we were the bottom
of the bowl, the sedimentary rock rolled

and the words were hulls of boats lapped by water.


38.

I walked around between classes imagining T4 counts,

two white-banded blue capsules every four hrs.

Later in the day, I rolled up my sleeve

and the nurse asked,
are you gay?
No.
Have you ever shared a needle with anyone?
No.
Have you had any intimate contact with anyone
who has AIDS or has been exposed to HIV?
No.
Sir, you need a psychiatrist, not a blood test.

39.

*Syphilis is a punishment God has reserved for our Late Ages* (Cotton Mather)

I'll take Defoe: "the fate of things gives a new face to things."

I plugged that into the '80s

after Jerry Falwell said: *AIDS is God's judgment for a society that does not live
    by His Rules—*


40.

The new Kinda Blue idea that Jerry claimed
came out of Cage with its modality of stretching time

with the Greek idea of fusing of color and sound

which is what I felt as I walked south after
the English department meeting—

into the hour when time becomes light:
the chalice of the Chrysler Building goes platinum,

the river starts dusting down
for bridge lights and traffic;

accretion, enumeration, excess
giving way to wrecked solitude

and an idea of late day
this day and after and after

after teaching, after the chalkboard
staring back at me

and light warping
through the glass of Grand Central:

everything goes Bohemian cobalt
Persian lapis, the Virgin's cloak—

color of longing over mountains—
that's how Miles drained his trumpet.


41.

aerosols, river haze, CS gas, we moved
with whatever floats—dispersions of self and industrial manna,
the shirtless exiles walking up 158th

along the river where your jewelry was stolen in an apartment
with jerry-rigged fire escapes, an inside job done by
mild-mannered tenants who disappeared into soot fumes

and the nanoparticles of spray-can mist;
by the time we realized what happened
they were in another state.


42.

At the Shadadeh Caves, where Armenians were asphyxiated in the summer
   of 1916,

we're filming, and M. is obsessed with light flickering down—
affect of the punctum:

while remaining a detail, the space fills up the whole picture.

M.: *Were thousands of Armenians stuffed in here?*
B.: *Fisk called them primitive gas chambers.*

M. drops the boom mic into darkness; sand floats through light-chipped space.

If you try to imagine death here, the detail is not the whole—the whole disappears.
The cave is a black gullet swallowing itself as it once did the bodies—


43.

David was living under scabs,
riveted by his past, and going north

on the A-Train I was reading
Defoe's *Journal of the Plague Year* :

following the London streets as they break apart into back alleys
and mews, intersecting circles, a broken lane sliced by
a carriage wheel—and there I found one intersection

between word and thing at Bishopsgate Cemetery
as it hooks into clumps of green before it's wiped out

by piles of rotting bodies and a compost of
souls who begat themselves to the other (London, 1720).

When I get out in the bright light of the sidewalk
words are dissolving into objects and air
and the DNA that's zinged by ultraviolet, infra-$Co_2$,

I scribbled in my Penguin edition:
"dangerous times/see clearly."

44.

Walking past the San Remo
that day, I was beginning to see history

as images filtered through cracked glass—
and then I heard sirens and watched a crowd

swell into the park.

Before the infrared spread over the mansard
of the Ansonia

I was back at the sink
my face slicing into surfaces
as the knife slits a kiwi

and the pubic fuzz
rubbed off in my palms

when it appeared on the screen:
Lennon's body on the sidewalk by the Dakota gate.

You called me from work,
your voice almost inaudible


45.

that's how the sound floated
in a noisy bistro—

the muted frequency froze me—
Jimmy Cobb's brushes were fine sand

blowing over glass—
blowing off into empty—

*slow and strange*, Count Basie said about *Kinda Blue*—
(not like the frantic bebop on-the-road).

It should be passé now
but the austere mute, wavering

alienated half-valves,
needled the nerves between two boroughs.

The glasses clink with various mediocre
wines; plates of poached salmon blur.


46.

By '83 T-cell syndrome was graffiti on the brain;

it wasn't a second Nineveh but still the zodiac read: Peking leprosy,
simian plague/Zaire/bubos/rat.


47.

Carrying in my hands dirt, rocks, bone fragments from the cave back to the van;

sun = total; Bedouin on the roadside herding sheep, women wrapped in black;

I'll tell you I was here but you won't believe me—and the camera crew wasn't
  imitating Orpheus.

48.

On Sunday—I stared at the closed curtain as the sharagans drifted into myrrh

under the gold-leaf Armenian dome on 34th and 2nd—
when you and Ani slept late—

*havedanius havedaneetz* to the memory of Anatolian church windows that had
    no glass
where the hawks glide out of the blue into the silver lamps

(the priest repeated the graffiti on the subway wall:
*Jesus hates corporate greed*).

The frankincense trailed me out to the street—

the dim sum already out,
the bad coffee drifting across 34th.

I slipped into a cab to the hospital
and was thinking about the


49.

via negativa—

feast on Grünewald's Christ,
ignominious, bitter, the lacerated skin,

dislocated joints on the rack,
gashes on the underside of the feet—

where the nails tore away the physics of the known—

take it beyond compassion and pity
to the awful real—


50.

Oil-rig flames in the distance on Iraqi border—
gray-violet light dissolves the desert and sense of order;

*Il y a longtemps que je t'aime*—

now the sky: black—and teal;
then the moon: vacant, white, unreal—


51.

That day as I was leaving—
David tossed me his amulet—

"Use it for me"—

I stared at *abra* and *cadabra*,
the lingering Aramaic

set into tesserae so the
word-sound could be action

and the sound-word could be hope.

I walked out of the hospital—
the air scrolled into itself,
the sky kissed my pores—

Who are you? the white bird asked,

*Less—*


52.

Carved head of Abraxas,
grazed it with my thumb:

head of a cock, body of a man,
serpent legs, wielding a club and shield.

The etched-away gold leaf
smooth and slightly ridged,

bought in a shop by Alan
(who died two years later) near the Park Hotel

where our great uncle from Buenos Aires introduced tango
to the Turks in '32, where Kemal

sat over gin and wine week after
week transfixed by the open
and closed embrace of the Argentine

2/4—4/4 as the seams of stockings
glazed the open floor and the neon
bar was almost lost in smoke.

I rubbed that Nilotic coin
into my thumb until the
two were one.

I wore it around my neck
in smog and sun.


53.

I still have the note Jerry left me on graph paper—
"In utter emptiness, anything can take place"—Cage.


54.

Half-light of morning
floating over the Euphrates;

long breath in: warm black:
slow breath out—cool blue.

If you feel the emptiness, you can see anything:
be in it: as matter, as matter of fact.

# THREE

## NO SIGN

1.

He: Is it night already?

She: No.

He: Did our house fall down?

She: What happened?

He: Is it you?

2.

He: Yes.

She: Why should I believe you?

He: Doesn't geology put us in our place?

              \*

He: We appeared in the age of fission:
vaporized bodies, ionized dragonflies, shadows printed on stone.

She: Japanese cities burned in my dreams.
       I saw the newsreels in class
decades later—

He: We're back here on the Palisades cliffs—staring at Manhattan—
    remember when the Sauternes was liquid gold?


3.

She: In the beginning there were alpha particles and gamma rays.

We always see daylight through the kitchen window near dusk
We can't forget how dusk turns the hydrangea deep blue.

We can't forget the glowing dioxin sun—the no-gaze,
morning bright blue agent-orange sky—even now—after all.


4.

He: Godard called *Hiroshima mon amour* Faulkner plus Stravinsky—

She: Remember: at the Angelika—September smell of light rain
warm sidewalks  shop awnings  late summer—

He: The noren curtains opened, the noren curtains closed.

We stared at kanji, birds, sketches of roofs, a tree

the lovers walked through the curtains either way

time shifted like breeze through eye sockets

She: They said goodbye and the noren curtains opened
and  the past was a  burning city
seen in silence, just images on screens.

*Lui: What did Hiroshima mean to you?*

*Elle: The end of the war, fear and terror that it could happen to us,
then indifference—astonishment that they dare do it—
then it became an unknown fear—*


5.

She: We're standing—

on an underground channel of molten rock
that fed volcanic eruptions 200 million years ago.

Earth = axis = spinning = two selves—swerve—possibility

He: Take Pan, all day we've played around with him.

She: Here we are—lying on Gaea.

He: Top of a volcano—molten basalt cooled and hardened
    we're on the sill still, and rock is never still—

She: The sill's eastern edge = Palisades cliffs, one version of home.


6.

He: Unified land mass—Pangea—Earth as whole—

She: Pan and Gaea = bridging self with other.

7.

He: Remember the blizzard of letters—commas,
question marks, dashes, words cut in half
on the subway walls at 4th—after we talked out the movie

you said—one view of the postwar:
a burger and a shake, a jukebox and a neon rainbow on the wall.


8.

He: If you said it was molten rock, I believed you.
If you said the molten rock was once underground

and created volcanic eruptions 200 million years ago,
I believed you.

If you said the eruptions covered 4 million square miles with
basalt lava, I didn't flinch.

And if the lava blasted gales of carbon dioxide and sulfur into the atmosphere,
I got the general idea.

I got the general idea that there were long volcanic winters after and after—

like sci-fi on a screen in a movie house at the beginning of time
when the reception was perfect.

She: Listen to Gaea: "We broke apart—200 million years ago—end of Triassic—

magma rose from deeper in the earth

intruded into the sandstones and shales, then the molten rock spread, cooled, hardened,
then—I was a sill overlaying softer rock—and the softer rock eroded."


9.

He: The look of ionized skin of the two lovers in bed
—the caressing, the trick of the camera

—irradiated light: those oboes and violins—and
the skeletal flutes—same as *Night and Fog*—

*Lui: You saw nothing.*
*Elle: I saw everything.*

*Elle: How could I have not seen it?*
*Lui: You saw nothing in Hiroshima.*


10.

She: Can you imagine the perfect eruptions until the clouds dissolved—
and the ocean became acidic like a whiteout gale and

the atmosphere heated up until most of life on Earth
was impossible?

Did you get the picture of Triassic extinction? Not many
creatures survived but giant lizards came to be the shape and form

we think of now when we take in this idea—even as the big screen breaks
down into a blank stare.

11.

He: Under the tulip trees in June

in the high grass of the Palisades

the sunlit bands across our bodies—

lying under the cicada-tree-rattling,
green-blur of leaves

dissolving into caterpillars—
chartreuse fur

and the violet flares of the sky—
we loved the hovering iridescent

dragonflies, a luna's green-wing
—the river water spilling

on the high grass
translucent moss on our backs.


12.

He: If you insist that the next 136 million years were dominated by the giant reptiles until an asteroid struck the place we now call Mexico

and the explosion ended the era of the lizards,
I can try to take that in—with or without the screen—

the imagination is limited even if we deny it.

13.

He: What Elle saw in the Hiroshima Peace Museum—what of it?

She: The illusion is also real—

what else can a tourist do but weep—
the burnt children in stupor like puppets—

city of ash and rubble, scorched metal.

He: Remember—Elle said: *I saw the newsreels on the second day*
the emphatic sensuality of her diction:
*deuxième jour, troisième jour, quinzième jour*—

you were pulled in by it.

She: I still love her.


14.

He: Am I still stuck to you?

like volcanic wetness,
like paint on canvass

pours, stick-wipes, splatters

She: I to you—in absence that kisses me—
thinned out on floors and boards,
like lava on flax—the glue of hands—

He: Craving for—sand, yolks, linseed oil—
soak the pulp as the Egyptians did—

15.

He: In the film it went like this:

*Lui: You made it all up*

*Elle: None of it*

*On the fifteenth day Hiroshima was covered with cornflowers and gladiolas, morning glories and daylilies—a strange fertility emerged*

*Lui: You made it all up*

*Elle: Just as the illusion exists in love—*
  *Those in the wombs of the women—*

Then Resnais' cut from deformed hands to her glistening fingers on his
  chest—

*Lui: Nothing. You know nothing—*


16.

She: inert gases—then
millions of years for oxygen to flow into it—

think of light as diffuse gamma rays spreading on the body of air—

He: Pan's idea of swamps coming into anthracite—fossilized
  leaf debris—

She: Gaea would say: detritus is a portrait of us.

17.

He: American implosion: the Conservatives need to deny history

She: Go back to Vietnam; the nation should have learned from it.


18.

He: I was your scent-carrier,

your rose-burning sun
we lived between hard rocks and clouds—

sussurring leaves licked us
crepuscular light loved us.

fading light over the Cloisters

everything dissolving into everything,
the bridge lights go on,

then the beyond: always implied by
the absence hanging over the cliffs.


19.

She: There was Dien Bien Phu—essential—
a ghost of grainy footage on some old reel

on which French soldiers slid down hillsides
like ants in glue—

the gray pixilated dissolve of 1954—the reality pill
down the hatch with no water—

He: refusal to learn from history.

She: Later—after Tet:

"We heard small Buddhist chimes ringing for peace in Hoa Bien."

Hanoi Nagasaki Saigon Hiroshima
Keep saying it—it will sink in.

2019—here— again—no light at end of the tunnel

No Sign—


20.

She: For hundreds of millions of years orogenic forces crushed
these stones—until they became mountains—that's Gaea's message:

millennia of abrasion from the ocean
decapitated headlands and broken rock.

He: We're standing on bloated eons of cliff crevice—

She: Rocks are time—(tell that to the fundamentalists)

feel them in your bones like a coal seam,
        the origin of the Hudson flowing down there
leaf debris
        pre-Cambrian stone
inscriptions beneath our feet.

21.

He: Who was there in the defoliated jungle,
the burning water spreading over bodies—

fuck // that was where Gaea and Pan
were supposed to hold hands

and walk across the DMZ ('68 Paris talks derailed)

that was the vision/wiped out/
by Nixon's scheme—for election = more

than a million dead.

She: Remember I loved you in the DMZ,
north and south, either/or
I loved you there—


22.

She: Forget about Gaea's offspring for now—

a creation myth is one way to understand
what the imagination reaches for—

He: We're here // facing something

                              we can't imagine—

23.

He: From the riverbank
the GW looked like a broken tower,

fog swallowing the vaults

light spilling out of clouds—

I saw cochineal birds
falling through bare steel, gray metallic
silver cables, nuts and bolts

—call it the functional sublime—blaring sheen

steel saddles holding giant barrel-cables

all night the humming in my head,

the burning tires going north to New England—


24.

He: As the fog blew off the bridge,

half-crocked,
we walked the deco gunmetal

following the flow of steel—

we ran all night under the fuselage-tubes vibrating over us—

who knew then the bridge was made of spun wires,
galvanized steel, 107,000 miles of it—enough to wrap
the globe 4 times—halfway to the moon (no metaphor)—

434 wires making up a strand of 3 inches—

anchorages tied the towers to the Palisades—
cut 45 feet down in the rock of the riverbed—

16 towers of steel floated on barges
June '28—Herbert Hoover's face

was bright; the moon passed between
Earth and the sun. The river was clear.

We sat at the edge looking down at the dark water.


25.

She: Between Can Tho and Saigon

*there were men in deep depression // manic nightmares*
*howling in mildew sheets.*

*Saigon was a final reel of* On the Beach, *a desolate city*
*whose long avenues held nothing but refuse, windblown papers,*
*small piles of human excrement, spent firecracker casings of the Lunar New Year.*

26.

He: After work, after sun-fade—

trucks and cars flow to Jersey and west—

the cables—joining dreamers—
stringer-lights flashing our faces.

We were lit up in T-shirts and jeans,
the West Side lighting the river,

the galvanized wires like magnetic fingertips
and plucks, guitar reverb distortion

overdrive—space between notes

a pistol shot, a siren.

Sometimes the whole bridge was a VST plug-in

amped in sync with untamable variations—(like Hendrix)
—flattened out cable distortion.

All night we bounced through falsetto plug-ins.


27.

She: translucent blur, shell fragments // white sparks smoke drift

the running tremor along the DMZ—

28.

She: Sometimes we were intimate, erotic, heat-waved
when the worst things were happening outside
in the big ugly world—our glass window on the Hudson
was a strange camera lens fading out the violence—
then we came and came to and got back out there.


29.

He: What caused the K-T mass extinction?

She: Darwin was aware of the discontinuity at the end of the Cretaceous—

He: Why is ocean acidification so dangerous?

She: "It changes the microbial communities"

toxic algae, falling ocean pH—$CO_2$—
impact of human greed = carbon fossil fuel fire—

He: You saw Paradise, California on fire; you saw Java and Sumatra
crash in the seismic sea—

read the sign—

She: Remember what Lucretius said:
"unless inclined to swerve all things would fall."

30.

She: Why are we hanging from this cliff
why these fragments—why these word-chips like mica—
like scree coming down now on us as we //

He: Look at the Hudson in the purple dusk,
when we can barely see the water, it's at fullest surge

—here and now—
spraying onto the rocks, driving
our gaze inward and out in one breath.


31.

He: No dream: the exit ramp at 175—we got
off the A-Train—blown away—under the silver sky

of the GW towers—the beacon lights sliding down
the cables—electric mist on my arms—

high-pass hum, no filter—

voltage of the insomniac walkway into the black—

distorted wave forms—it's what I'm after—non-
linear currents—

a revenant hand on the keyboard
just valve overdrive, a cathode unstrung—

light-spots  shadow-tips  sundial traces—
big zoom purple fringing everywhere—

(magenta ghosts you called them)

under the cloudy stars—the wind-spray
drench of evening brought me back to you—

running through a wall of sound
a vacuum tube—

strung out on a geodesic curve.


32.

*Lui: Nothing, you know nothing*

*Elle: Food became an object of fear*

*Lui: You don't know what it is to forget*

*Elle: No, you are not endowed with memory*

*Lui: Like you I longed for a memory beyond consolation*

*Elle: Against the horror of no longer understanding*

*Lui: A memory of shadows and stone*

*Elle: I have struggled not to forget*

33.

She: And now. The inconceivable,
    with Trump everything's a moving target—
including the Earth—

He: Trump signing Bibles after a tornado in Alabama—

She: the price of losing reality.


34.

He: After we split—I lived for
days under the sunsets of Zaum

sky above—bridge below.
If the shortest route between ends
is a single point where light meets—

then purple fringing along the river
was my site line and I lived in it for a while

watching the lights of the distant Triboro
and flashing reds of the airport—

headlights of cars going west—

the black ribbon of route 80 vanishing from the bridge lights
to the Water Gap—

breathing the buzzing air
fretboard cables—trusses, plate girders—wires—

35.

She: Remember the shadow cast by the sun, axial spin of Earth—

time // stone // self = postmodern homo sapiens—

remember the heat of the pre-Cambrian sun remember Pangaea.

36.

He: When will the sun bloat into a red giant—after the oceans are boiled away and the Earth is bleached—

She: But now Sauternes light coming down over the Palisades

Solid to liquid to gas—$H_2O$—to $CO_2$—

tree as life—

Pan meeting Gaea.

37.

He: Remember—the air was still, trees motionless, the sky touched my chest—here at the rocks on the river edge I came to feel:

—how does the soul speak?

Does it come out of the blue or out of some recondite preparation—unknown to us in day?

38.

She: I was under the illusion that I will never forget Hiroshima.

He: The flash was a giant yellow light—*bokuzuki* were useless
the houses in the neighborhood evaporated—

She: The illusion of history is so perfect that the tourists cry.

He: What else can a tourist do?


39.

She: We're heating up—biotic attrition is just a euphemism

a quarter of all species heading into the black hole—

He: what about the phyla of books, music, art, zigzag of buildings-to-God
    going in the slow ash—


40.

She: "Nothing can be brought back into nothingness nor be created
                             out of naught" (Lucretius)

He: "Who teaches the soul?" (Juan de la Cruz)—

how the daemon comes and goes not like a bolt
but like the breeze of a curtain opening.

41.

He: As for radioactive dating of rock; rethink mile-stones = milestones—
          life in hand—

bronze light of late day off the river—
the momentary sheen—

She: Signifying something between souls.
Love is both: the seam and the rock.

Dusk turns the hydrangeas deep blue.


42.

He: I rowed under the sunlit towers of the bridge,

light pouring down on the concrete vaults
magenta birds diving into the sun-bubbling waves—

tugs and barges fading into gold haze.


43.

She: Think of Monet painting blind the emptiness of blue.

Top of the skull rises into the smoke from distant Queens

into the lily pond of the sky,
smooth brush of horizon.

Van Gogh said absolute black does not exist—
keep in mind—his joy—in the purple shadow moving over us

as the dark comes—just
as now the black silhouettes of Shadow Man
are visible in the night facades—


44.

He: I know beneath this hull is rift and subduction
underwater jazz and terror—as if Sun Ra and Chopin embraced
beneath a surface they didn't understand—

She:—remember: light spills as dark comes—chalk floats off the silhouettes.


45.

*Lui: You saw nothing.*

*Elle: I saw everything.*

*Lui: What did it mean to you?*

The curtains are always moving—
light turns the hydrangea deep blue.

# NOTES ON THE TEXT

Thank you to the following publications, in which versions of these poems first appeared:

*AGNI*: sections 1–33 and 42–43 of "A-Train / Ziggurat / Elegy"
*Carolina Quarterly*: section 33 of "Ozone Journal" (as "Waking/West End Ave./1983")
*Saveur*: section 12 of "Ozone Journal" (as "Breakfast in Aleppo")
*Slate*: section 38 of "A-Train / Ziggurat / Elegy" (as "Blue")
*Virginia Quarterly Review*: section 45 of "Ozone Journal" (as "Kinda Blue")

The poem "No Sign" in a slightly earlier version was published in a limited edition in 2020 by Arrowsmith Press (Cambridge, MA).

"A-Train / Ziggurat / Elegy": The following sources were helpful and quoted passages self-evident: P. R. S. Moorey's *Ur "of The Chaldees": A Revised and Updated Edition of Sir Leonard Woolley's "Excavations at Ur"*; Angus K. Gillespie's *Twin Towers: The Life of New York City's World Trade Center*; Eric Darton's *Divided We Stand: A Biography of New York's World Trade Center*; and Anthony Aveni's *Empires of Time: Calendars, Clocks, and Cultures*. Section 42: Italicized lines are from Walt Whitman's "Drum-Taps: First O Songs for a Prelude."

"Ozone Journal": The following sources were helpful and are quoted in the designated sections: Section 11: John Cage's *Indeterminacy*; Section 17: Annika Nilsson's *Ultraviolet Reflections*; Section 34: Walter Benjamin's "Theses on the Philosophy of History" (from *Illuminations*); Section 43: Daniel Defoe's *A Journal of the Plague Year*; Section 48: *havedanius havedaneetz*, Armenian, "unto eternity of eternities" (from the closing of the Lord's Prayer); Section 53: John Cage's "For a Speaker" (from *Silence*); Susan Sontag's *Illness as Metaphor*.

In the spring of 2009, I went with a TV crew from CBS's *60 Minutes* to do a segment on the Armenian genocide and to search for human remains in the Der Zor desert of eastern Syria, where more than four hundred thousand Armenians died of famine and massacre at the hands of the Turkish killing squads in 1915. One thread of "Ozone Journal" borrows from that experience as the Syrian desert becomes a point of perspective for the persona's "dreaming back."

Jerry in "Ozone Journal" is based on the pioneering jazz and blues producer and music executive George Avakian (1919–2017). As a junior at Yale in 1940, Avakian produced for Decca Records the first ever jazz LP, *Chicago Jazz*, and shortly after produced LP boxed sets of Louis Armstrong, Fletcher Henderson, Billie Holiday, and others for Columbia Records. In 2012, with Michael Coyle and Kara Rusch, I conducted twelve hours of interviews with Avakian.

Sections 5, 27, 31, and 36: for George Avakian.
Sections 40 and 45: for Michael Coyle and Kara Rusch.

"No Sign": The following sources were helpful in writing the designated sections: Sections 19, 25, and 28: Michael Herr's *Dispatches*; Sections 20 and 37: Paul Pinet's *Shadowed by Deep Time*; Section 30: Lucretius's *The Nature of Things* (trans. A. E. Stallings); Sections 30, 40, and 42: Elizabeth Kolbert's *The Sixth Extinction*; Section 39: John Hersey, *Hiroshima*; Section 43: "Shadow Man" refers to the street artist Richard Hambleton. Italicized lines are from the film *Hiroshima mon amour*, script by Marguerite Duras and Alan Resnais.

Gratitude to George Avakian, Mary Behrens, Bruce Berlind, Sven Birkerts, Jennifer Brice, Michael Coyle, Doris Cross, Donna Frieze, Robert Garland, Rachel Goshgarian, Karen Harpp, Ed Harris, Walter Kalaidjian, Helen Kebabian, Mary Beth Kelly, Denise Leone, Matt Leone, B. J. Lifton, Robert Jay Lifton, Askold Melnyczuk, Angela Miller, John Naughton, Randy Petilos, Jane Pinchin, Robert Pinsky, Wendy Ranan, Kara Rusch, Eric Simonoff, Tom Sleigh, Bruce Smith, Chuck Strozier, Chris Tilghman, the Wellfleet Meetings, Jack Wheatcroft, and Yaddo.